Goat Skill

T0337597

Contents

Written by Isabel Thomas

Collins

Goats have skills

Goats look a bit like sheep.

smooth coat

wool

But goats have some skills that sheep
do not have.

Goats get up high!

What a sight!

Goats can get up trees.

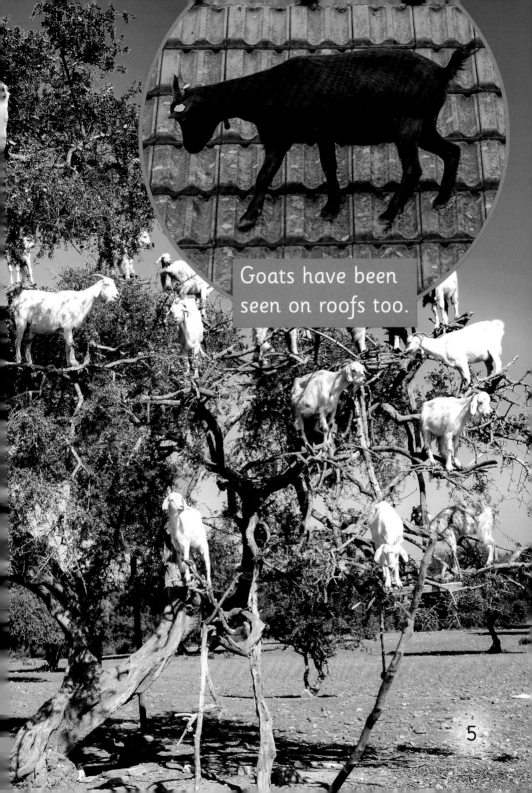

Goats have been seen on roofs too.

Some goats can get high up cliffs and **crags**!

This goat is in the **Alps**.

Zoom in on a goat's **hoof**. It can grip tight.

7

Non-stop munching!

Goats feed on greens ...

but they will munch lots of odd things too.

Some goats think rubbish is food!

Goats can go!

Goats can run and **trot**.

They are good at jumping too.

A goat's jump
can be as long as
three goats!

Sight skills

Goats have fantastic sight.

The odd slits help them to see well at night.

But to a goat, red looks like green.

Digging goats

Some goats sleep in pits!

The goat digs a pit in the dust.
It rests and **grooms** its coat in the pit.

Goats have big brains!

Goats like to be pals with us!

They can tell when we are glad or sad.

Goats run to us if they get a fright.

If a goat has a problem, they look at us and **coax** us to help!

Glossary

Alps high land

coax win our help

crags rocks and hills

grooms gets mess off

hoof foot

trot quick running

Index

Goat skills

getting up high

munching

jumping

22

seeing

hanging out with us

digging

23

 After reading

Letters and Sounds: Phases 3 and 4

Word count: 216

Focus phonemes: /ch/ /sh/ /th/ /ng/ /ai/ /ee/ /igh/ /oa/ /oo/ /oo/, and adjacent consonants

Common exception words: of, to, the, are, we, be, they, have, like, do, some, when, out, what, our, go

Curriculum links: Science: Animals, including humans

National Curriculum learning objectives: Reading/word reading: read accurately by blending sounds in unfamiliar words containing GPCs that have been taught; read common exception words, noting unusual correspondences between spelling and sound and where these occur in a word; read other words of more than one syllable that contain taught GPCs; Reading/comprehension (KS2): understand what they read, in books they can read independently, by checking that the text makes sense to them, discussing their understanding and explaining the meaning of words in context; identifying main ideas drawn from more than one paragraph and summarising these

Developing fluency

- Read pages 2 and 3 aloud to your child, demonstrating an enthusiastic tone.
- Take turns to read the rest of the book, checking that your child does not miss the labels and captions.

Phonic practice

- Point to the following words with adjacent consonants with long vowel sounds. Ask your child to sound them out and then blend them.

  page 2: smooth (*s/m/oo/th*) page 4: trees (*t/r/ee/s*)
  page 18: fright (*f/r/igh/t*)

- Turn to pages 10 and 11 and challenge your child to find, sound out and read more words with adjacent consonants. (*trot, jumping, jump, three*)

Extending vocabulary

- Ask your child to suggest a word or phrases with opposite meanings (antonyms) for these words from the glossary:

  o grooms (e.g. *messes up, makes dirty*)

  o trot (e.g. *crawl, walk slowly*)